Thomas Jefferson

written by **Joeming Dunn**
illustrated by **Rod Espinosa**

magic wagon

visit us at
www.abdopublishing.com

Published by Magic Wagon, a division of the ABDO Publishing Group, 8000 West 78th Street, Edina, Minnesota 55439. Copyright © 2009 by Abdo Consulting Group, Inc. International copyrights reserved in all countries. All rights reserved. No part of this book may be reproduced in any form without written permission from the publisher.
Graphic Planet™ is a trademark and logo of Magic Wagon.

Printed in the United States.

Written by Joeming Dunn
Illustrated by Rod Espinosa
Edited by Stephanie Hedlund and Rochelle Baltzer
Interior layout and design by Antarctic Press
Cover art by Rod Espinosa
Cover design by Neil Klinepier

Library of Congress Cataloging-in-Publication Data

Dunn, Joeming.
    Thomas Jefferson / written by Joeming Dunn ; illustrated by Rod Espinosa.
        p. cm. -- (Bio-graphics)
    Includes index.
    ISBN 978-1-60270-174-8
    1. Jefferson, Thomas, 1743-1826--Juvenile literature. 2. Presidents--United States--Biography--Juvenile literature. I. Espinosa, Rod. II. Title.
E332.79.E87 2009
973.4'6092--dc22
    [B]   2007051502

TABLE of CONTENTS

Timeline

1743 - Thomas Jefferson was born at Shadwell, Virginia, on April 13.

1769 - Jefferson was elected to the Virginia House of Burgesses.

1772 - On January 1, Jefferson married Martha Wayles Skelton.

1775 - Jefferson was elected to the Second Continental Congress.

1776 - Jefferson drafted the Declaration of Independence.

1797-1801 - Jefferson served as vice president of the United States.

1801-1809 - Jefferson was the third president of the United States.

1803 - The United States purchased land from France in the Louisiana Purchase.

1819-1825 - The University of Virginia was built with the help of Jefferson.

1826 - Thomas Jefferson died at Monticello on July 4.

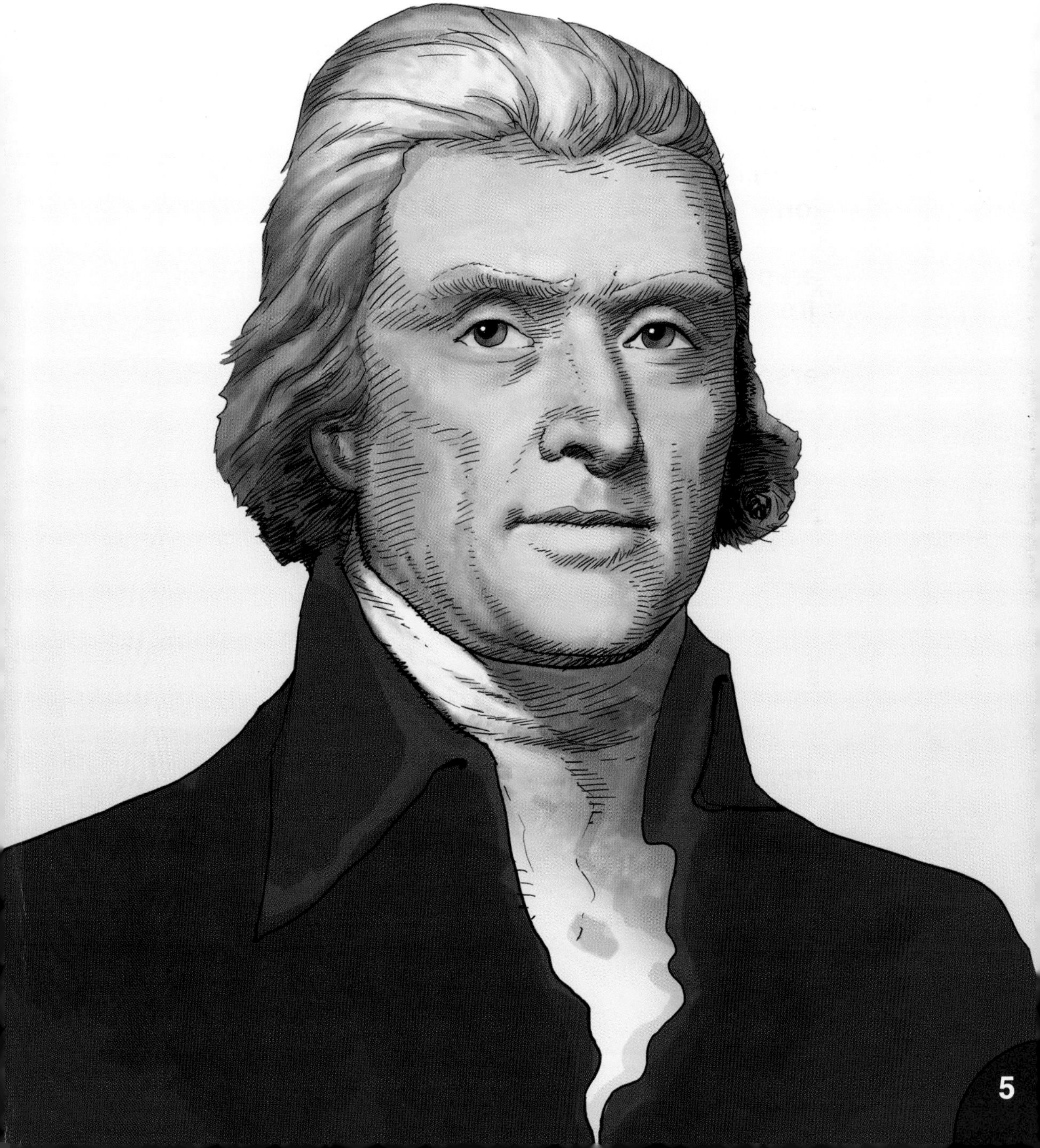

Thomas Jefferson was born on April 13, 1743, in Shadwell, Virginia. His parents were Peter Jefferson, a landowner, and Jane Randolph Jefferson.

LET'S NAME HIM THOMAS.

THOMAS JEFFERSON. THAT'S A NICE NAME.

Young Thomas was curious about the world around him. He read often and was interested in music. He grew into a tall young man.

Thomas went to the College of William and Mary from 1760 to 1762. He studied law.

STUDYING LAW WILL ENABLE ME TO HELP OTHERS IN NEED.

In 1770, Thomas inherited 5,000 acres of land. He began building his own home on that land.

WHAT WILL YOU CALL YOUR NEW HOME, TOM?

I WAS THINKING OF... MONTICELLO.

From 1769 to 1775, Thomas served as a representative in the Virginia House of Burgesses. He was known for his ability with words.

DAY BY DAY, ENGLAND ROBS US OF OUR FREEDOM. NOW, THEY CAN ARREST ANYONE AT ANY TIME.

Thomas married a widow named Martha Wayles Skelton on January 1, 1772.

THIS IS OUR NEW HOME, MONTICELLO. PARTS OF IT ARE NOT YET FINISHED, BUT ENOUGH OF IT IS FOR US TO LIVE IN.

IT'S BEAUTIFUL!

Thomas and Martha had six children. Only Mary and Martha survived past the age of two.

I'M GETTING TIRED, FATHER. CAN I PLAY NOW?

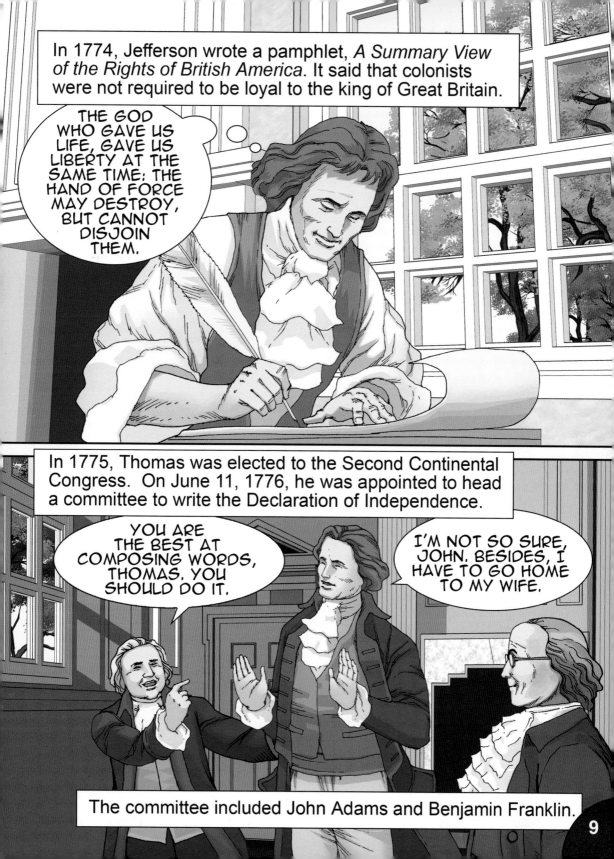

In 1774, Jefferson wrote a pamphlet, *A Summary View of the Rights of British America*. It said that colonists were not required to be loyal to the king of Great Britain.

THE GOD WHO GAVE US LIFE, GAVE US LIBERTY AT THE SAME TIME; THE HAND OF FORCE MAY DESTROY, BUT CANNOT DISJOIN THEM.

In 1775, Thomas was elected to the Second Continental Congress. On June 11, 1776, he was appointed to head a committee to write the Declaration of Independence.

YOU ARE THE BEST AT COMPOSING WORDS, THOMAS. YOU SHOULD DO IT.

I'M NOT SO SURE, JOHN. BESIDES, I HAVE TO GO HOME TO MY WIFE.

The committee included John Adams and Benjamin Franklin.

Working with Franklin and Adams, Jefferson wrote the original draft of the Declaration of Independence.

MAYBE YOU CAN PUT IN A REFERENCE TO OWING NO ALLEGIANCES TO KINGS.

YOU SHOULD ALSO INCLUDE THAT ALL MEN SHOULD BE FREE.

The Declaration was submitted to Congress.

GENTLEMEN, I PRESENT TO YOU THE DECLARATION OF INDEPENDENCE!

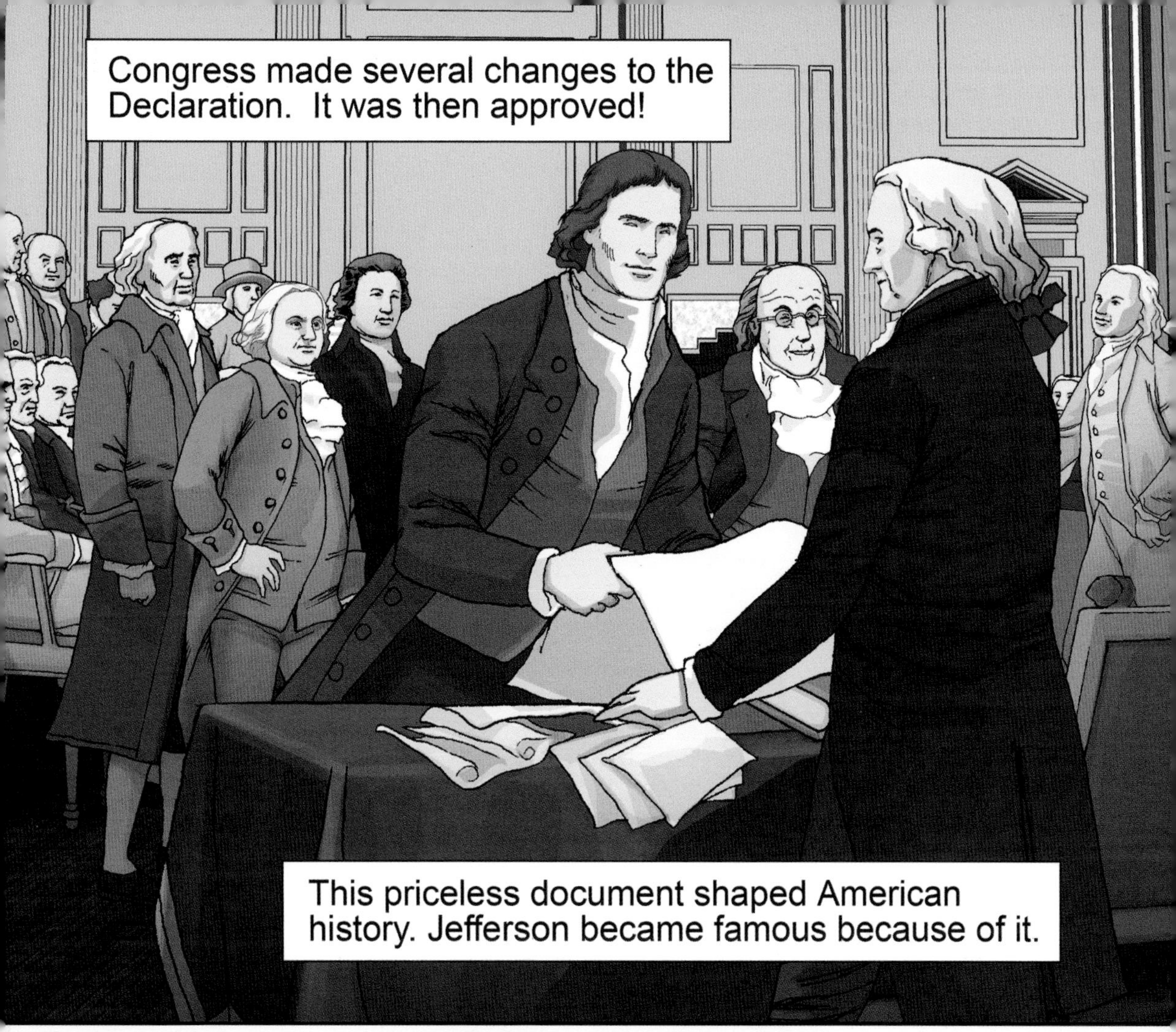
Congress made several changes to the Declaration. It was then approved!
This priceless document shaped American history. Jefferson became famous because of it.

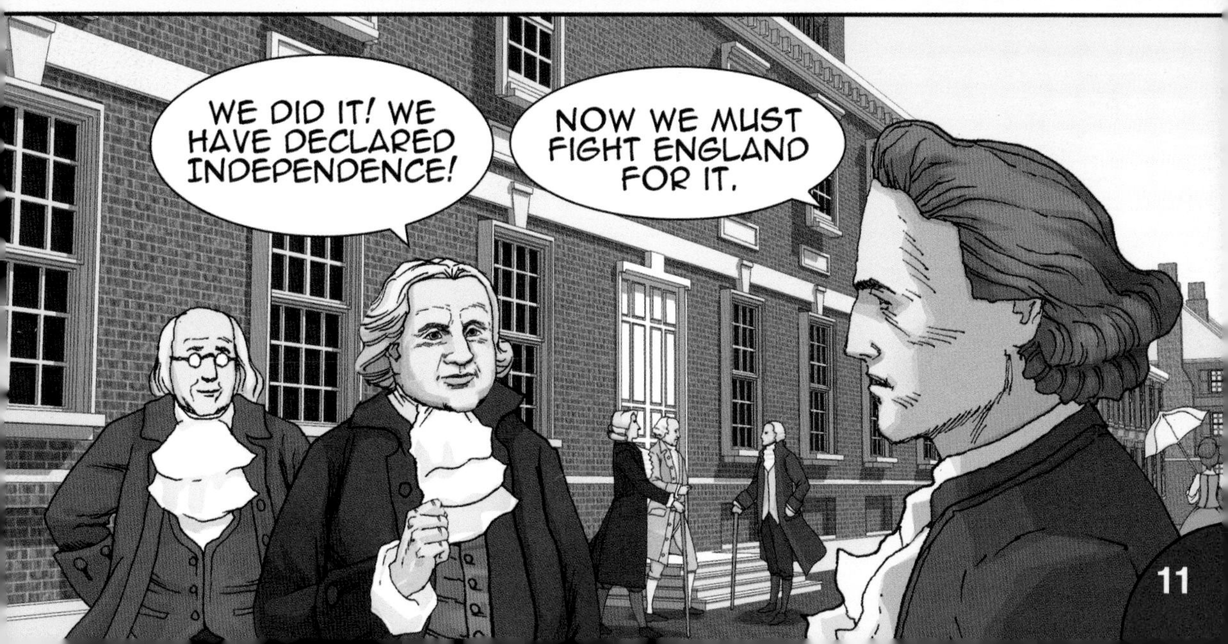
WE DID IT! WE HAVE DECLARED INDEPENDENCE!
NOW WE MUST FIGHT ENGLAND FOR IT.

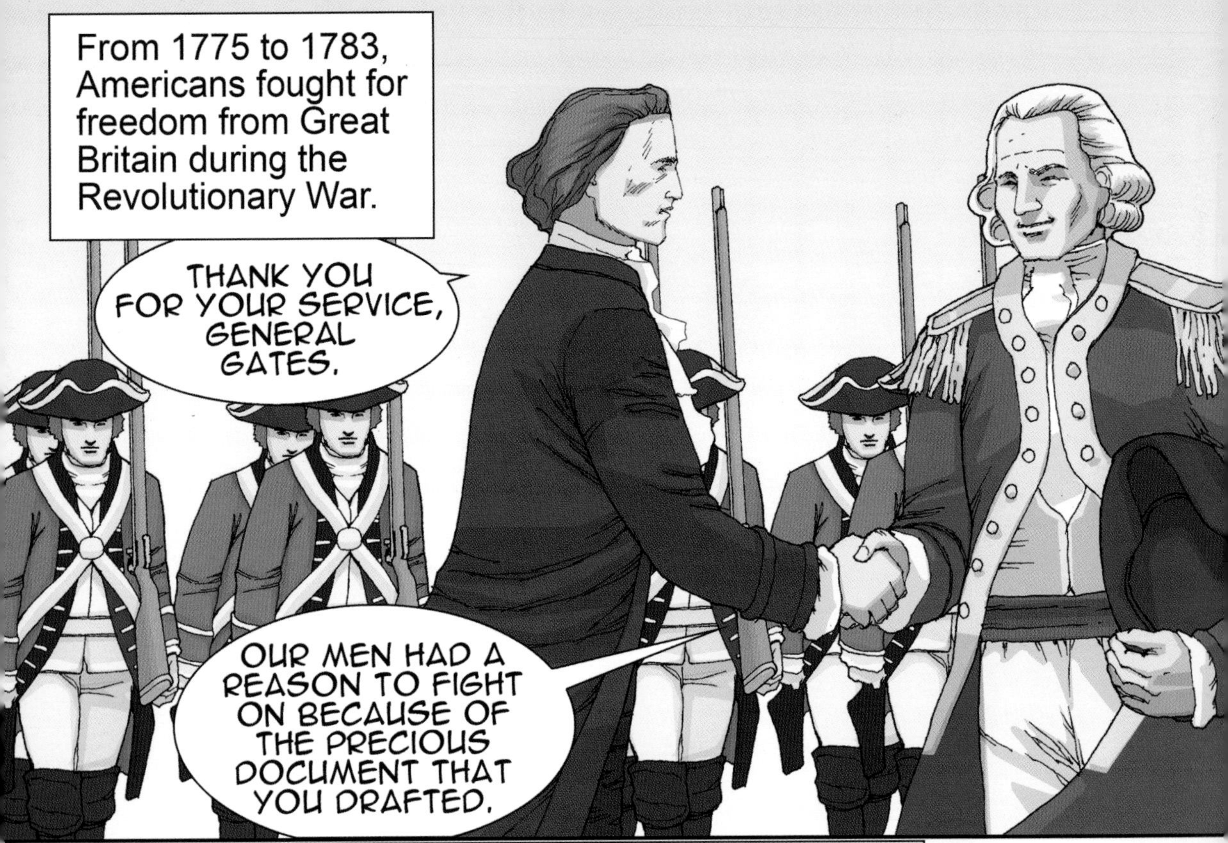
From 1775 to 1783, Americans fought for freedom from Great Britain during the Revolutionary War.
THANK YOU FOR YOUR SERVICE, GENERAL GATES.
OUR MEN HAD A REASON TO FIGHT ON BECAUSE OF THE PRECIOUS DOCUMENT THAT YOU DRAFTED.

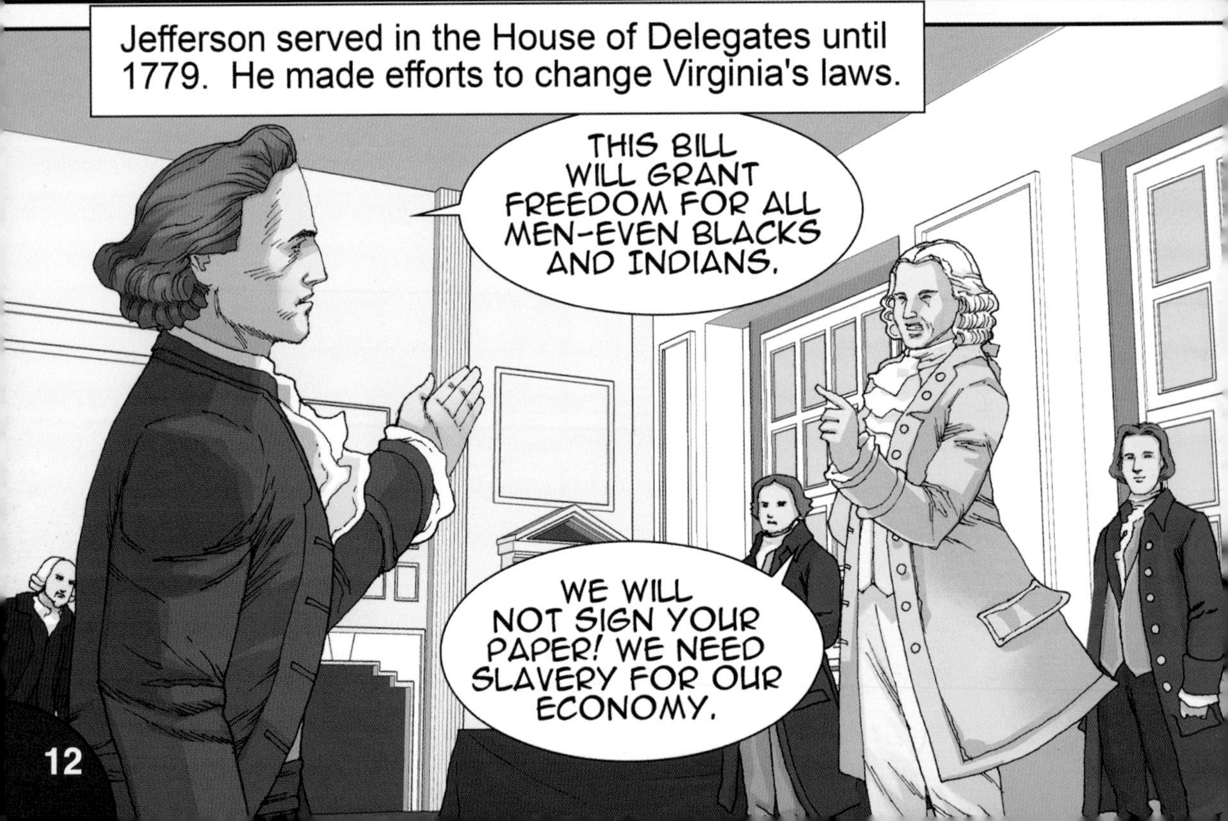
Jefferson served in the House of Delegates until 1779. He made efforts to change Virginia's laws.
THIS BILL WILL GRANT FREEDOM FOR ALL MEN-EVEN BLACKS AND INDIANS.
WE WILL NOT SIGN YOUR PAPER! WE NEED SLAVERY FOR OUR ECONOMY.

In June 1779, Jefferson introduced a bill for religious freedom.

... ALL MEN SHALL BE FREE TO PROFESS, AND BY ARGUMENT TO MAINTAIN, THEIR OPINIONS ON MATTERS OF RELIGION.

THAT'S WELL WRITTEN, THOMAS!

This bill caused resistance for many years. With help from James Madison, it was finally ratified in 1786.

THE FREEDOM OF RELIGION SHOULD BE A FUNDAMENTAL RIGHT OF ALL AMERICANS.

Chapter 3 *Governor Jefferson*

In June 1779, Jefferson was elected governor of Virginia. His administration was constantly criticized.

THEY SAY I AM A COWARD FOR RUNNING AWAY.

A MAN WHO RUNS AWAY LIVES TO FIGHT ANOTHER DAY.

He retired from his position as governor in June 1781.

FINALLY, I CAN GO HOME...

Jefferson's wife, Martha, died on September 6, 1782. This deeply affected Jefferson.

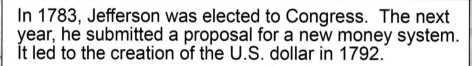

In 1783, Jefferson was elected to Congress. The next year, he submitted a proposal for a new money system. It led to the creation of the U.S. dollar in 1792.

Jefferson also proposed a law that gave all states the same benefits and rights. Before this, new states did not have the same rights as the original 13 states.

Jefferson continued to work to abolish slavery. Although he was a slave owner, he believed the system should not be allowed to spread.

YOU SAY YOU ARE AGAINST SLAVERY, BUT ARE YOU NOT ALSO A SLAVE OWNER, SIR?

I HAVE RESOLVED LONG AGO TO SET MY SLAVES FREE.

Plantation owners who did not agree with slavery treated their slaves with kindness. Some of them feared that if they released their slaves others may subject them to harsh treatment.

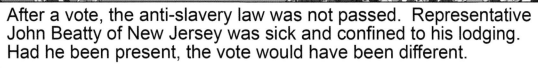

After a vote, the anti-slavery law was not passed. Representative John Beatty of New Jersey was sick and confined to his lodging. Had he been present, the vote would have been different.

THE LAW BANNING SLAVERY HAS BEEN VOTED ON AND THE MAJORITY SAYS "NAY."

Jefferson found other causes to support.

MAYBE I CAN HELP WITH FOREIGN RELATIONS...

In 1784, Thomas Jefferson was sent to Paris, France, to help negotiate treaties. In 1785, he took over the post of minister to France from Benjamin Franklin.

FRANKLIN HAS SERVED US WELL. I HOPE TO CONTINUE HIS WORK.

He followed the events in America closely. He advised that the United States have a bill of rights.

I FEEL DISCONNECTED HERE, BEING SO FAR FROM OUR COUNTRY.

OUR COUNTRY NEEDS US HERE TO CONTINUE TALKING TO THE FRENCH.

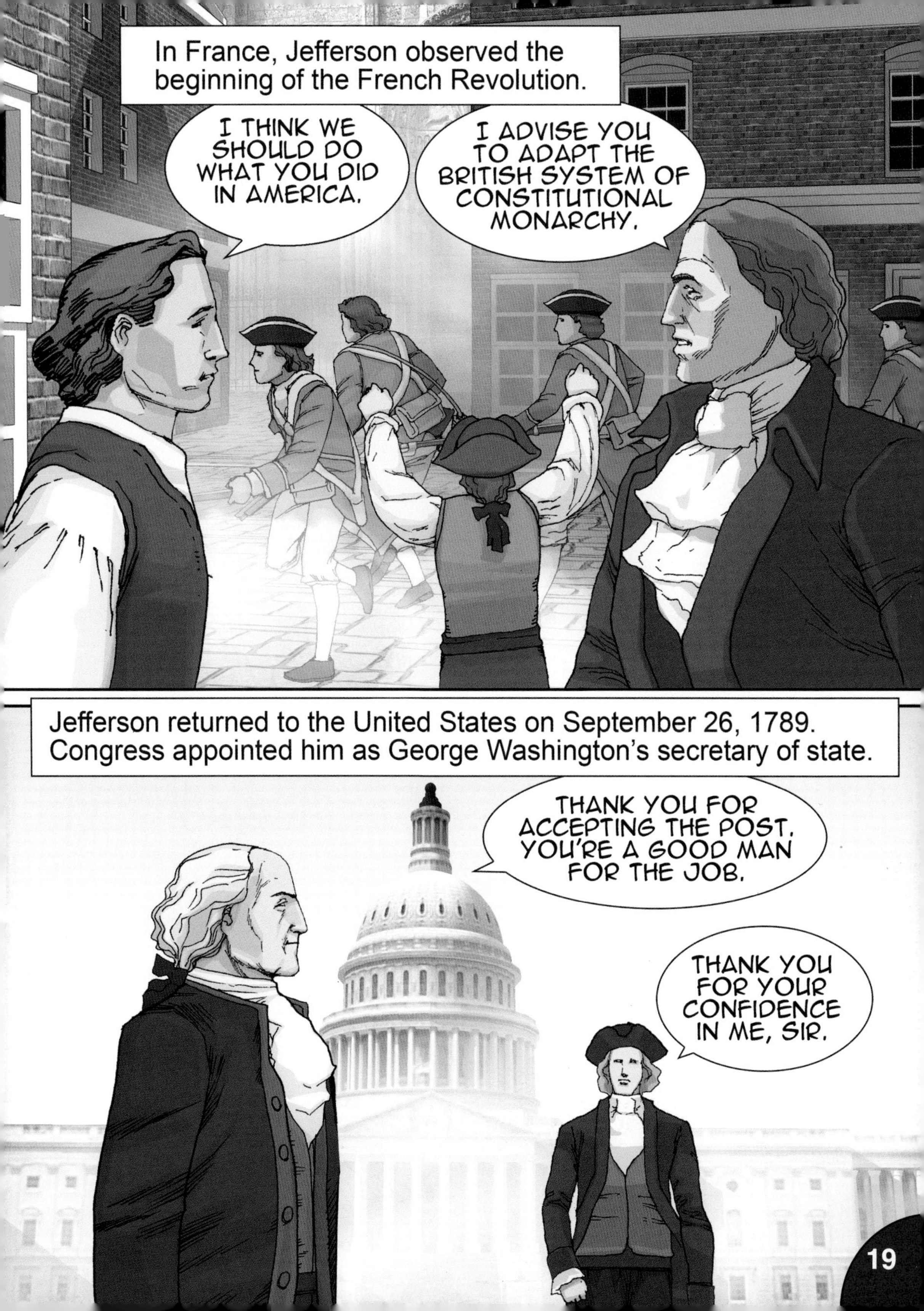
In France, Jefferson observed the beginning of the French Revolution.
I THINK WE SHOULD DO WHAT YOU DID IN AMERICA.
I ADVISE YOU TO ADAPT THE BRITISH SYSTEM OF CONSTITUTIONAL MONARCHY.
Jefferson returned to the United States on September 26, 1789. Congress appointed him as George Washington's secretary of state.
THANK YOU FOR ACCEPTING THE POST. YOU'RE A GOOD MAN FOR THE JOB.
THANK YOU FOR YOUR CONFIDENCE IN ME, SIR.

At home, he fought against lawmakers who were inserting monarchist amendments into the new country's laws.

THE UNITED STATES OF AMERICA SHOULD NOT HAVE LAWS THAT WOULD ALLOW KINGS OR ANY FORM OF ROYALTY TO RULE OVER US.

Jefferson retired on December 31, 1793. As secretary of state, he had served his country with honor.

For the next three years, Jefferson devoted his efforts to his family and improving his farm. He designed an experimental plow. He also built a nail factory.

THE NAIL FACTORY WILL BE BUILT OVER THERE. WE START TOMORROW.

YES, MR. JEFFERSON.

He welcomed both local and foreign guests into his home. His grandchildren visited him often.

WELCOME TO MONTICELLO.

THANK YOU.

Despite being retired, he followed events in the country.

THE WHISKEY REBELLION COULD HAVE BEEN HANDLED BETTER, I THINK.

In 1796, John Adams became the president of the United States. Jefferson was elected his vice president.

During his term, Jefferson continued to fight for the freedom of the Americas.

OUR YOUNG DEMOCRACY DOES NOT NEED LAWS THAT WOULD REDUCE THE FREEDOM OF OUR PEOPLE.

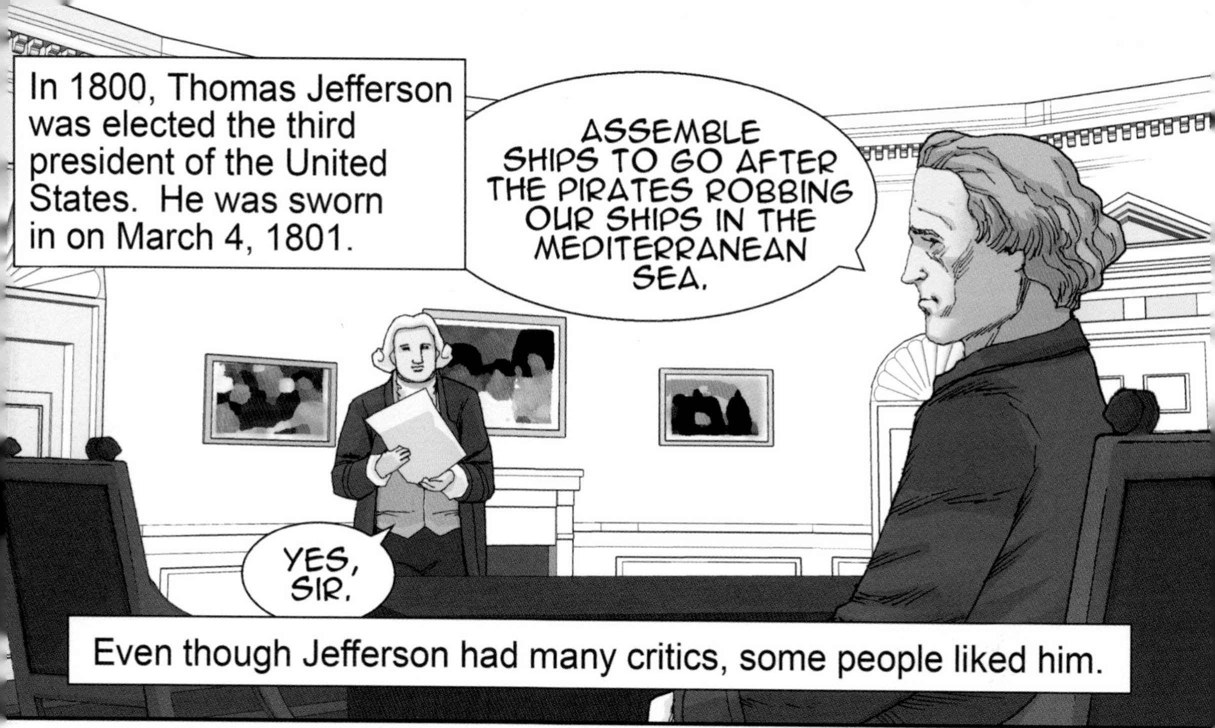
In 1800, Thomas Jefferson was elected the third president of the United States. He was sworn in on March 4, 1801.
ASSEMBLE SHIPS TO GO AFTER THE PIRATES ROBBING OUR SHIPS IN THE MEDITERRANEAN SEA.
YES, SIR.
Even though Jefferson had many critics, some people liked him.

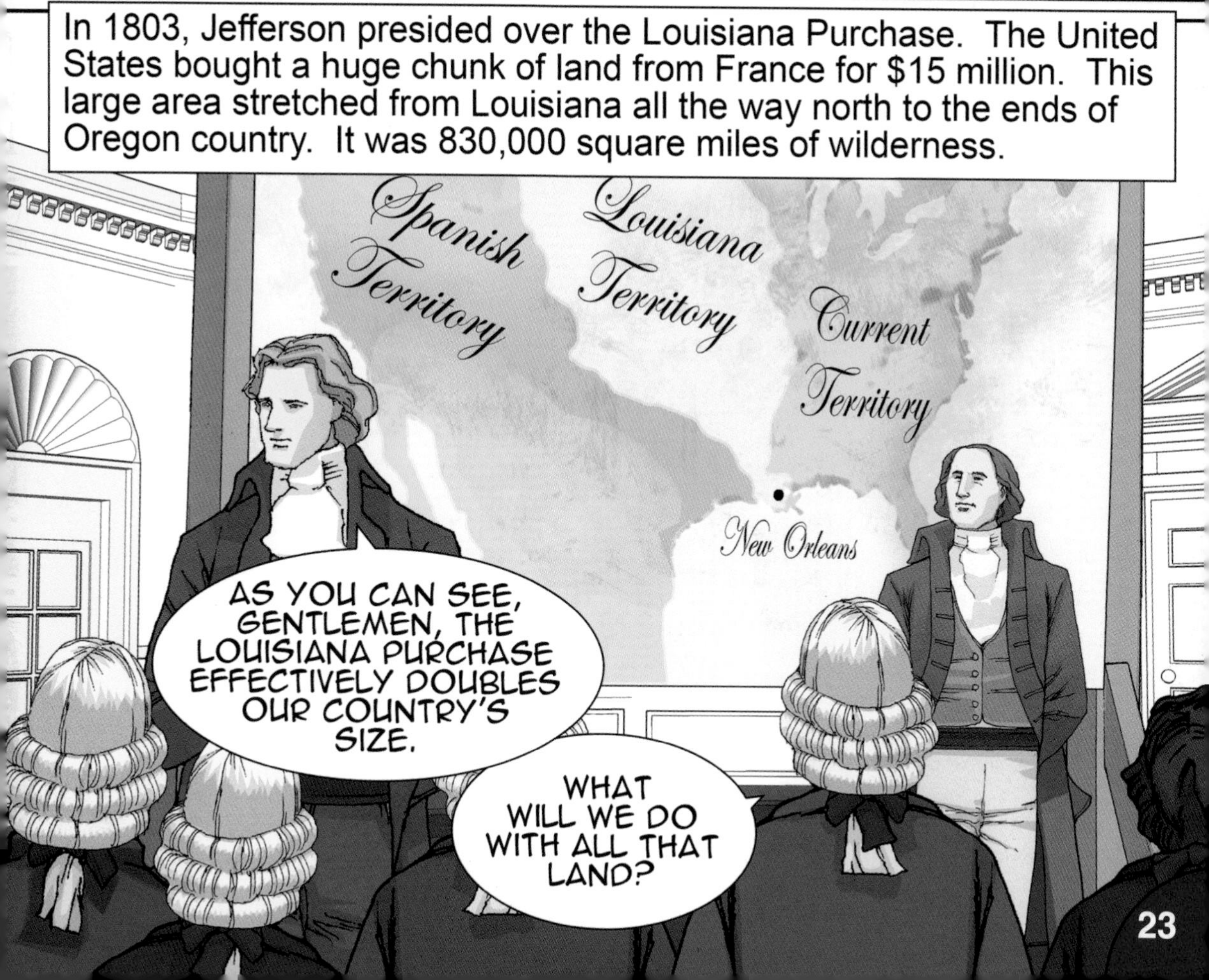
In 1803, Jefferson presided over the Louisiana Purchase. The United States bought a huge chunk of land from France for $15 million. This large area stretched from Louisiana all the way north to the ends of Oregon country. It was 830,000 square miles of wilderness.
Spanish Territory
Louisiana Territory
Current Territory
New Orleans
AS YOU CAN SEE, GENTLEMEN, THE LOUISIANA PURCHASE EFFECTIVELY DOUBLES OUR COUNTRY'S SIZE.
WHAT WILL WE DO WITH ALL THAT LAND?

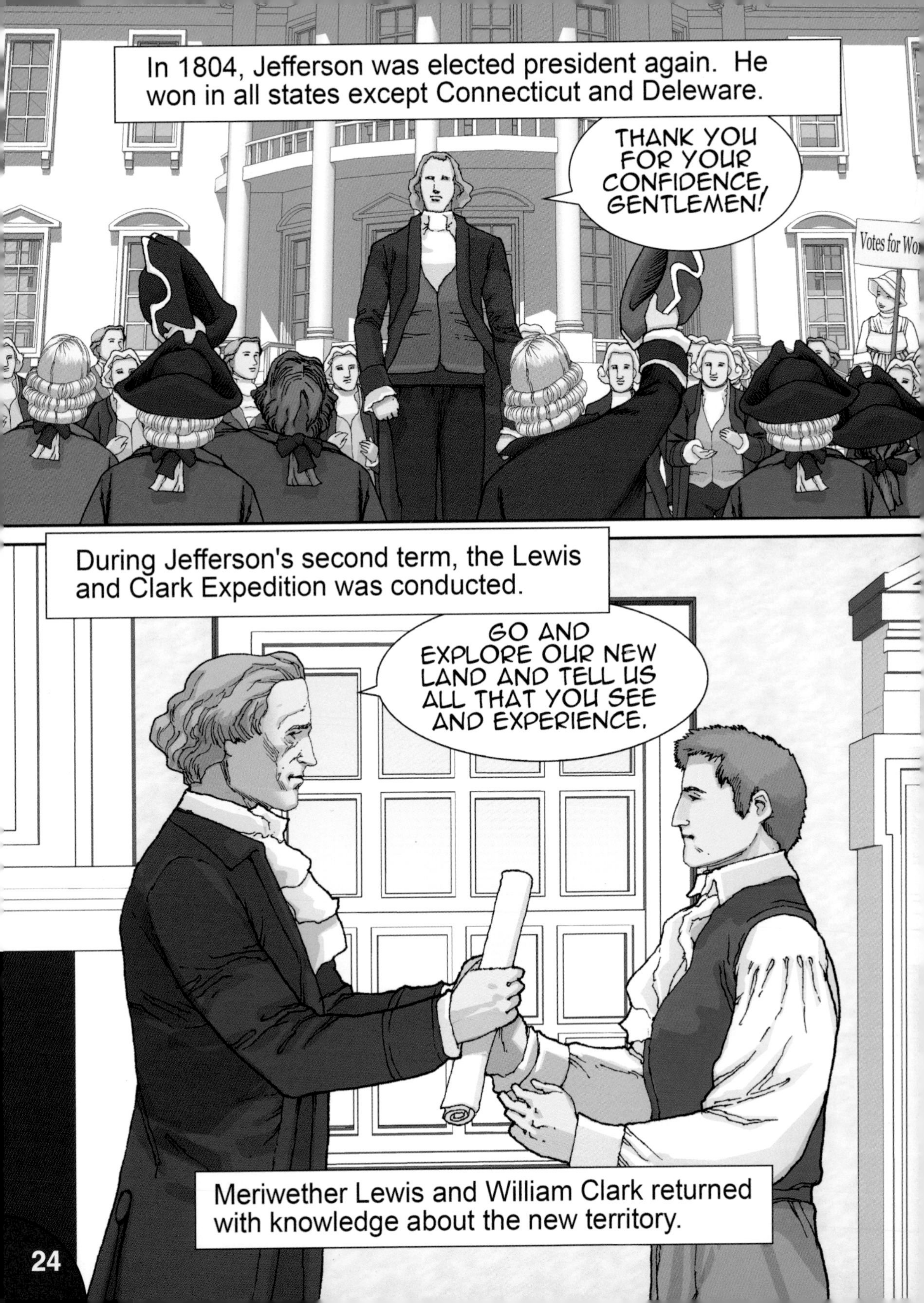
In 1804, Jefferson was elected president again. He won in all states except Connecticut and Deleware.
THANK YOU FOR YOUR CONFIDENCE, GENTLEMEN!
During Jefferson's second term, the Lewis and Clark Expedition was conducted.
GO AND EXPLORE OUR NEW LAND AND TELL US ALL THAT YOU SEE AND EXPERIENCE.
Meriwether Lewis and William Clark returned with knowledge about the new territory.

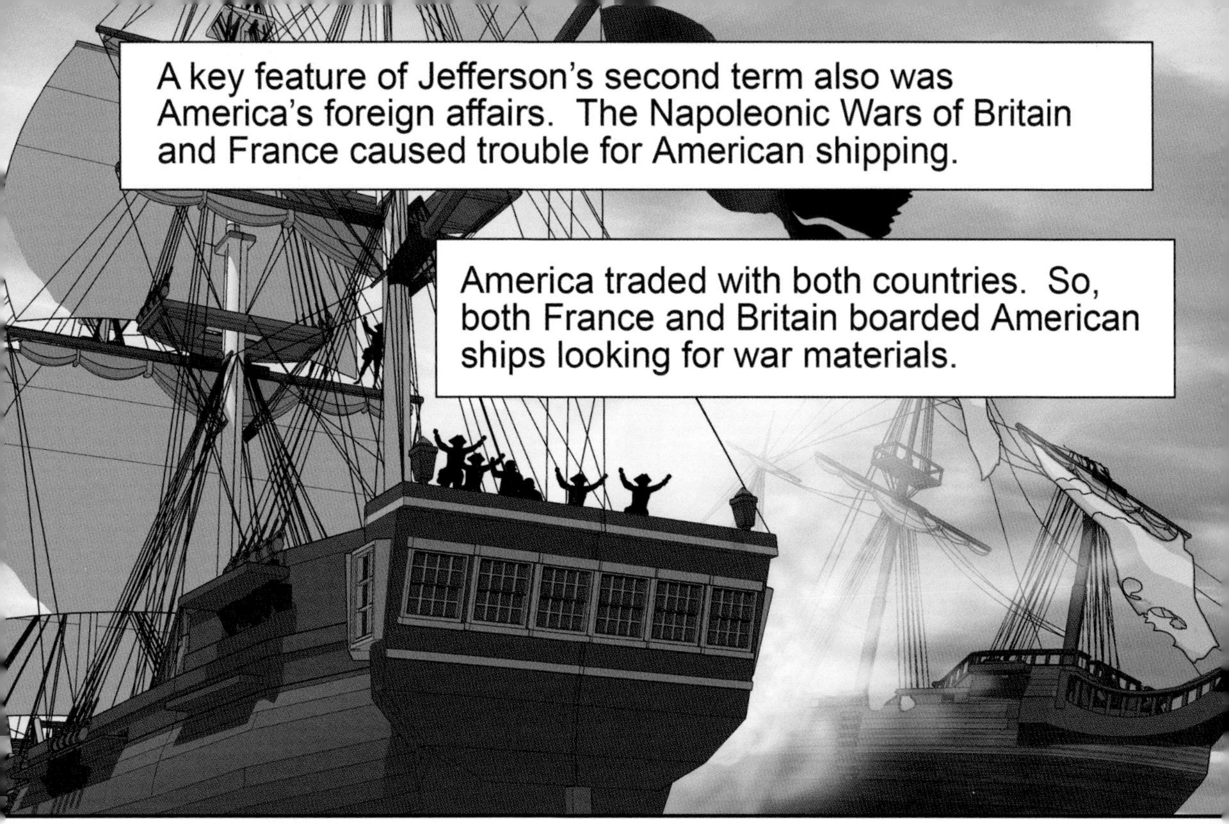
A key feature of Jefferson's second term also was America's foreign affairs. The Napoleonic Wars of Britain and France caused trouble for American shipping.
America traded with both countries. So, both France and Britain boarded American ships looking for war materials.

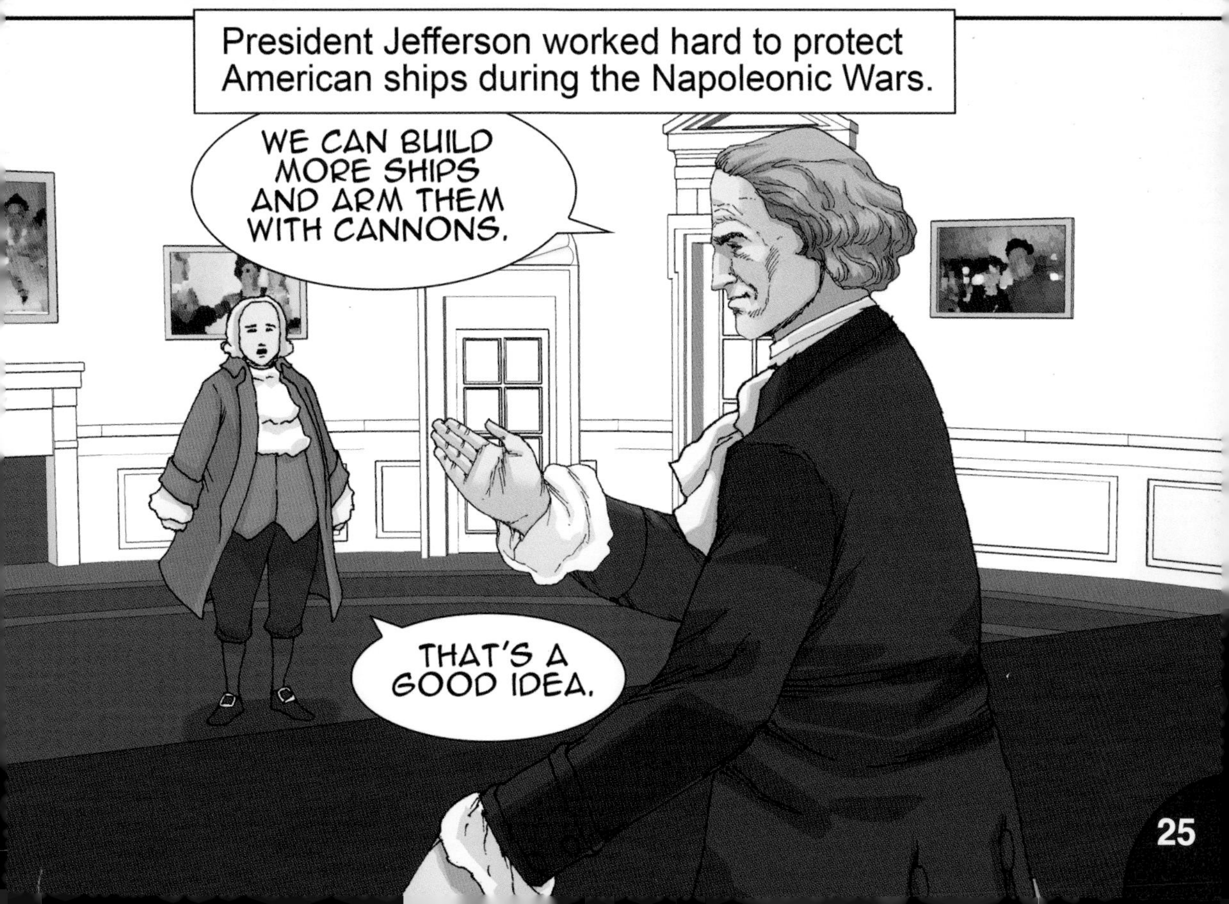
President Jefferson worked hard to protect American ships during the Napoleonic Wars.
WE CAN BUILD MORE SHIPS AND ARM THEM WITH CANNONS.
THAT'S A GOOD IDEA.

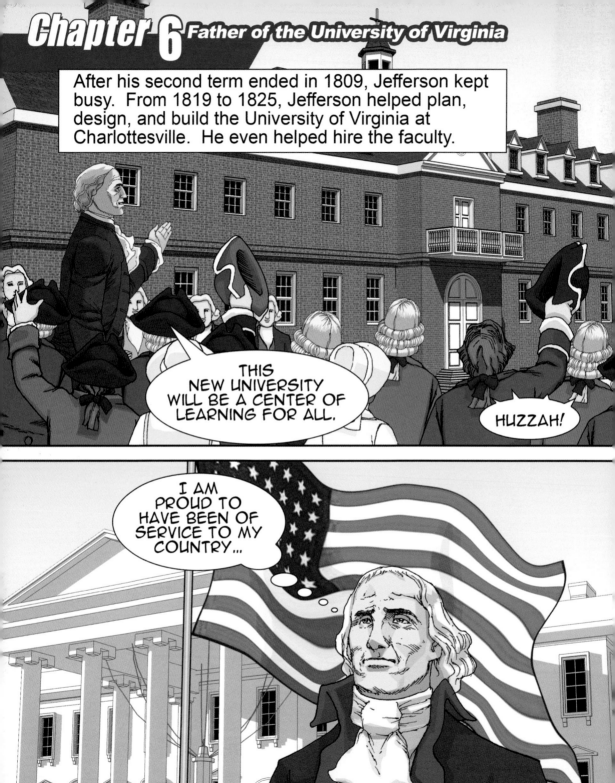

After his second term ended in 1809, Jefferson kept busy. From 1819 to 1825, Jefferson helped plan, design, and build the University of Virginia at Charlottesville. He even helped hire the faculty.

THIS NEW UNIVERSITY WILL BE A CENTER OF LEARNING FOR ALL.

HUZZAH!

I AM PROUD TO HAVE BEEN OF SERVICE TO MY COUNTRY...

Thomas Jefferson and John Adams corresponded often in retirement. They shared their memories of their younger days as Founding Fathers.

They were the only two Declaration of Independence signers who became president.

THOSE WERE THE DAYS, EH, THOMAS? YOU ALMOST REFUSED TO WRITE THE DECLARATION.

TO THINK I ALMOST MISSED THAT OPPORTUNITY. THANK GOODNESS YOU INSISTED I DO IT.

On July 4, 1826, Thomas Jefferson died at Monticello. It was the fiftieth anniversary of the Declaration of Independence.

Jefferson's contributions shaped the United States of America. His legacy will last forever.

HERE WAS BURIED
THOMAS JEFFERSON
AUTHOR OF THE
DECLARATION
OF
AMERICAN INDEPENDENCE
OF THE
STATUTE OF VIRGINIA
FOR
RELIGIOUS FREEDOM
AND FATHER OF THE
UNIVERSITY OF VIRGINIA

IN CONGRESS, JULY 4, 1776.

The unanimous Declaration of the thirteen united States of America,

When, in the course of human events, it becomes necessary for one people to dissolve the political bonds which have connected them with another, and to assume among the powers of the earth, the separate and equal station to which the laws of nature and of nature's God entitle them, a decent respect to the opinions of mankind requires that they should declare the causes which impel them to the separation.

We hold these truths to be self-evident, that all men are created equal, that they are endowed by their Creator with certain unalienable rights, that among these are life, liberty and the pursuit of happiness. That to secure these rights, governments are instituted among men, deriving their just powers from the consent of the governed. That whenever any form of government becomes destructive to these ends, it is the right of the people to alter or to abolish it, and to institute new government, laying its foundation on such principles and organizing its powers in such form, as to them shall seem most likely to effect their safety and happiness. Prudence, indeed, will dictate that governments long established should not be changed for light and transient causes; and accordingly all experience hath shown that mankind are more disposed to suffer, while evils are sufferable, than to right themselves by abolishing the forms to which they are accustomed. But when a long train of abuses and usurpations, pursuing invariably the same object evinces a design to reduce them under absolute despotism, it is their right, it is their duty, to throw off such government, and to provide new guards for their future security. --Such has been the patient sufferance of these colonies; and such is now the necessity which constrains them to alter their former systems of government. The history of the present King of Great Britain is a history of repeated injuries and usurpations, all having in direct object the establishment of an absolute tyranny over these states. To prove this, let facts be submitted to a candid world.

He has refused his assent to laws, the most wholesome and necessary for the public good. He has forbidden his governors to pass laws of immediate and pressing importance, unless suspended in their operation till his assent should be obtained; and when so suspended, he has utterly neglected to attend to them. He has refused to pass other laws for the accommodation of large districts of people, unless those people would relinquish the right of representation in the legislature, a right inestimable to them and formidable to tyrants only. He has called together legislative bodies at places unusual, uncomfortable, and distant from the depository of their public records, for the sole purpose of fatiguing them into compliance with his measures. He has dissolved representative houses repeatedly, for opposing with manly firmness his invasions on the rights of the people. He has refused for a long time, after such dissolutions, to cause others to be elected; whereby the legislative powers, incapable of annihilation, have returned to the people at large for their exercise; the state remaining in the meantime exposed to all the dangers of invasion from without, and convulsions within. He has endeavored to prevent the population of these states; for that purpose obstructing the laws for naturalization of foreigners; refusing to pass others to encourage their migration hither, and raising the conditions of new appropriations of lands. He has obstructed the administration of justice, by refusing his assent to laws for establishing judiciary powers. He has made judges dependent on his will alone, for the tenure of their offices, and the amount and payment of their salaries. He has erected a multitude of new offices, and sent hither swarms of officers to harass our people, and eat out their substance. He has kept among us, in times of peace, standing armies without the consent of our legislature.

He has affected to render the military independent of and superior to civil power. He has combined with others to subject us to a jurisdiction foreign to our constitution, and unacknowledged by our laws; giving his assent to their acts of pretended legislation: For quartering large bodies of armed troops among us: For protecting them, by mock trial, from punishment for any murders which they should commit on the inhabitants of these states: For cutting off our trade with all parts of the world: For imposing taxes on us without our consent: For depriving us in many cases, of the benefits of trial by jury:

For transporting us beyond seas to be tried for pretended offenses: For abolishing the free system of English laws in a neighboring province, establishing therein an arbitrary government, and enlarging its boundaries so as to render it at once an example and fit instrument for introducing the same absolute rule in these colonies: For taking away our charters, abolishing our most valuable laws, and altering fundamentally the forms of our governments: For suspending our own legislatures, and declaring themselves invested with power to legislate for us in all cases whatsoever. He has abdicated government here, by declaring us out of his protection and waging war against us. He has plundered our seas, ravaged our coasts, burned our towns, and destroyed the lives of our people. He is at this time transporting large armies of foreign mercenaries to complete the works of death, desolation and tyranny, already begun with circumstances of cruelty and perfidy scarcely paralleled in the most barbarous ages, and totally unworthy the head of a civilized nation. He has constrained our fellow citizens taken captive on the high seas to bear arms against their country, to become the executioners of their friends and brethren, or to fall themselves by their hands. He has excited domestic insurrections amongst us, and has endeavored to bring on the inhabitants of our frontiers, the merciless Indian savages, whose known rule of warfare, is undistinguished destruction of all ages, sexes and conditions. In every stage of these oppressions we have petitioned for redress in the most humble terms: our repeated petitions have been answered only by repeated injury. A prince, whose character is thus marked by every act which may define a tyrant, is unfit to be the ruler of a free people. Nor have we been wanting in attention to our British brethren. We have warned them from time to time of attempts by their legislature to extend an unwarrantable jurisdiction over us. We have reminded them of the circumstances of our emigration and settlement here. We have appealed to their native justice and magnanimity, and we have conjured them by the ties of our common kindred to disavow these usurpations, which, would inevitably interrupt our connections and correspondence. We must, therefore, acquiesce in the necessity, which denounces our separation, and hold them, as we hold the rest of mankind, enemies in war, in peace friends.

We, therefore, the representatives of the United States of America, in General Congress, assembled, appealing to the Supreme Judge of the world for the rectitude of our intentions, do, in the name, and by the authority of the good people of these colonies, solemnly publish and declare, that these united colonies are, and of right ought to be free and independent states; that they are absolved from all allegiance to the British Crown, and that all political connection between them and the state of Great Britain, is and ought to be totally dissolved; and that as free and independent states, they have full power to levy war, conclude peace, contract alliances, establish commerce, and to do all other acts and things which independent states may of right do. And for the support of this declaration, with a firm reliance on the protection of Divine Providence, we mutually pledge to each other our lives, our fortunes and our sacred honor.

Button Gwinnett
Lyman Hall
Geo Walton.

Wm Hooper
Joseph Hewes
John Penn

Edward Rutledge

Thos Heyward Junr.
Thomas Lynch Junr.
Arthur Middleton

John Hancock

Samuel Chase
Wm Paca
Thos Stone
Charles Carroll of Carrollton

George Wythe
Richard Henry Lee
Th Jefferson
Benja Harrison
Thos Nelson jr.
Francis Lightfoot Lee
Carter Braxton

Robt Morris
Benjamin Rush
Benja Franklin
John Morton
Geo Clymer
Jas Smith
Geo Taylor
James Wilson
Geo Ross
Caesar Rodney
Geo Read
Tho McKean

Wm Floyd
Phil Livingston
Frans Lewis
Lewis Morris

Richd Stockton
Jno Witherspoon
Fras Hopkinson
John Hart
Abra Clark

Josiah Bartlett
Wm Whipple
Saml Adams
John Adams
Robt Treat Paine
Elbridge Gerry
Step Hopkins
William Ellery
Roger Sherman
Saml Huntington
Wm Williams
Oliver Wolcott
Matthew Thornton

29

Further Reading

Kallen, Stuart A. *Thomas Jefferson*. Founding Fathers series. Edina: ABDO Publishing Company, 2001.

Mullin, Rita Thievon. *Thomas Jefferson: Architect of Freedom*. New York: Sterling Publishing Company, 2007.

Nardo, Don. *Thomas Jefferson*. Danbury: Scholastic Library Publishing, 2003.

Welsbacher, Anne. *Thomas Jefferson*. The United States Presidents. Edina: ABDO Publishing Company, 1999.

Glossary

amendment - a change to a country's constitution.

constitutional monarchy - a form of government ruled by a monarch who must follow the laws of a constitution.

criticize - to find fault with something. People who voice their opinions are called critics.

French Revolution - from 1789 to 1799, a major transformation of France's society from a monarchy to a republic of free citizens.

Louisiana Purchase - land the United States purchased from France in 1803. It extended from the Mississippi River to the Rocky Mountains and from Canada to the Gulf of Mexico.

Napoleonic Wars - a series of wars fought in Europe from 1800 to 1815.

pamphlet - a printed publication without a cover.

ratify - to officially approve.

Web Sites

To learn more about Thomas Jefferson, visit ABDO Publishing Company on the World Wide Web at **www.abdopublishing.com.** Web sites about Jefferson are featured on our Book Links page. These links are routinely monitored and updated to provide the most current information available.

Index